Baby Pandas
at the Zoo

Eustacia Moldovo

 Enslow Publishing
101 W. 23rd Street
Suite 240
New York, NY 10011
USA
enslow.com

Published in 2016 by Enslow Publishing, LLC.
101 W. 23rd Street, Suite 240, New York, NY 10011

Library of Congress Cataloging-in-Publication Data
Moldovo, Eustacia.
Baby pandas at the zoo / Eustacia Moldovo.
  pages cm. — (All about baby zoo animals)
Audience: Age 4-6.
Audience: K to Grade 3.
Includes bibliographical references and index.
Summary: "Describes the life of a panda cub at a zoo, including its behaviors, diet, and physical traits"— Provided by publisher.
ISBN 978-0-7660-7079-0 (library binding)
ISBN 978-0-7660-7077-6 (pbk.)
ISBN 978-0-7660-7078-3 (6-pack)
1. Pandas—Infancy—Juvenile literature. 2. Zoo animals—Juvenile literature. I. Title.
QL795.P18M65 2016
599.789'139—dc23

                    2015000149

Printed in the United States of America

To Our Readers: We have done our best to make sure all Web sites in this book were active and appropriate when we went to press. However, the author and the publisher have no control over and assume no liability for the material available on those Web sites or on any Web sites they may link to. Any comments or suggestions can be sent by e-mail to customerservice@enslow.com.

Photo Credits: Aaron Ferster/Science Source/Getty Images, pp. 4–5; bendao/Shutterstock.com, p. 20; Eastimages/Shutterstock.com, pp. 3 (left), 14; flySnow/iStock/Thinkstock, p. 1; enmyo/Shutterstock.com, pp. 8, 18; Hung Chung Chih/Shutterstock.com, p. 11; Kitch Bain/Shutterstock.com, p. 6; silverjohn/Shutterstock.com, pp. 3 (center), 16, 22; Sue Bishop/Oxford Scientific/Getty Images, pp. 3 (right), 12.

Cover Credits: silverjohn/Shutterstock.com (sleeping panda in tree); Nelson Marques/Shutterstock.com (baby blocks on spine).

Contents

Words to Know.................... 3

Who Lives at the Zoo? 5

Read More 24

Web Sites 24

Index 24

Words to Know

bamboo   **cub**   **paw**

Who lives at the zoo?

Smithsonian
National
Zoological
Park

Hours
May 1 to September 15
Grounds: 4:30 am to 8:00 pm
Buildings: 10:00 am to 6:00 pm

September 16 to April 30

A baby panda lives at the zoo!

A baby panda is called a cub.

Panda cubs are black and white. A panda cub's thick fur keeps it warm.

A panda cub's paw has five fingers and a thumb. This helps it hold bamboo.

A panda cub eats a lot of bamboo. In a zoo, a panda cub eats carrots, apples, and rice too.

A panda cub climbs trees to stay safe from danger. It can also swim!

A panda cub lives with its mother at the zoo. They talk to each other by roaring, growling, and honking.

Panda cubs do not move around much. They eat or sleep most of the day.

You can see a panda cub
at the zoo!

Read More

Hanson, Anders. *Panda*. Edina, Minn.: ABDO Publishing, 2014.

Ryder, Joanne. *Panda Kindergarten*. New York: HarperCollins, 2015.

Web Sites

National Geographic Kids: Giant Panda
  kids.nationalgeographic.com/content/kids/en_US/animals/giant-panda/

San Diego Zoo Kids: Giant Panda
  kids.sandiegozoo.org/animals/mammals/giant-panda

Index

bamboo, 13, 15

cub, 9, 11, 13, 15, 17, 19, 21, 23

eat, 15, 21

fur, 11

mother, 19

paw, 13

sleep, 21

swim, 17

trees, 17

zoo, 5, 7, 15, 19, 23

Guided Reading Level: C
Guided Reading Leveling System is based on the guidelines recommended by Fountas and Pinnell.

Word Count: 126